DOCTOR WHO

BBC

THE TARDIS

2013
DIARY

MALLON
Melbourne

DOCTOR WHO

BBC

2013

DIARY

POLICE PUBLIC CALL BOX

2013

JANUARY

M	T	W	T	F	S	S
	1	2	3	4	5	6
7	8	9	10	11	12	13
14	15	16	17	18	19	20
21	22	23	24	25	26	27
28	29	30	31			

FEBRUARY

M	T	W	T	F	S	S
				1	2	3
4	5	6	7	8	9	10
11	12	13	14	15	16	17
18	19	20	21	22	23	24
25	26	27	28			

MARCH

M	T	W	T	F	S	S
				1	2	3
4	5	6	7	8	9	10
11	12	13	14	15	16	17
18	19	20	21	22	23	24
25	26	27	28	29	30	31

APRIL

M	T	W	T	F	S	S
1	2	3	4	5	6	7
8	9	10	11	12	13	14
15	16	17	18	19	20	21
22	23	24	25	26	27	28
29	30					

MAY

M	T	W	T	F	S	S
		1	2	3	4	5
6	7	8	9	10	11	12
13	14	15	16	17	18	19
20	21	22	23	24	25	26
27	28	29	30	31		

JUNE

M	T	W	T	F	S	S
					1	2
3	4	5	6	7	8	9
10	11	12	13	14	15	16
17	18	19	20	21	22	23
24	25	26	27	28	29	30

JULY

M	T	W	T	F	S	S
1	2	3	4	5	6	7
8	9	10	11	12	13	14
15	16	17	18	19	20	21
22	23	24	25	26	27	28
29	30	31				

AUGUST

M	T	W	T	F	S	S
			1	2	3	4
5	6	7	8	9	10	11
12	13	14	15	16	17	18
19	20	21	22	23	24	25
26	27	28	29	30	31	

SEPTEMBER

M	T	W	T	F	S	S
30						1
2	3	4	5	6	7	8
9	10	11	12	13	14	15
16	17	18	19	20	21	22
23	24	25	26	27	28	29

OCTOBER

M	T	W	T	F	S	S
	1	2	3	4	5	6
7	8	9	10	11	12	13
14	15	16	17	18	19	20
21	22	23	24	25	26	27
28	29	30	31			

NOVEMBER

M	T	W	T	F	S	S
				1	2	3
4	5	6	7	8	9	10
11	12	13	14	15	16	17
18	19	20	21	22	23	24
25	26	27	28	29	30	

DECEMBER

M	T	W	T	F	S	S
30	31					1
2	3	4	5	6	7	8
9	10	11	12	13	14	15
16	17	18	19	20	21	22
23	24	25	26	27	28	29

2014

JANUARY

M	T	W	T	F	S	S
		1	2	3	4	5
6	7	8	9	10	11	12
13	14	15	16	17	18	19
20	21	22	23	24	25	26
27	28	29	30	31		

FEBRUARY

M	T	W	T	F	S	S
					1	2
3	4	5	6	7	8	9
10	11	12	13	14	15	16
17	18	19	20	21	22	23
24	25	26	27	28		

MARCH

M	T	W	T	F	S	S
					1	2
3	4	5	6	7	8	9
10	11	12	13	14	15	16
17	18	19	20	21	22	23
24	25	26	27	28	29	30
31						

APRIL

M	T	W	T	F	S	S
	1	2	3	4	5	6
7	8	9	10	11	12	13
14	15	16	17	18	19	20
21	22	23	24	25	26	27
28	29	30				

MAY

M	T	W	T	F	S	S
			1	2	3	4
5	6	7	8	9	10	11
12	13	14	15	16	17	18
19	20	21	22	23	24	25
26	27	28	29	30	31	

JUNE

M	T	W	T	F	S	S
						1
2	3	4	5	6	7	8
9	10	11	12	13	14	15
16	17	18	19	20	21	22
23	24	25	26	27	28	29
30						

JULY

M	T	W	T	F	S	S
	1	2	3	4	5	6
7	8	9	10	11	12	13
14	15	16	17	18	19	20
21	22	23	24	25	26	27
28	29	30	31			

AUGUST

M	T	W	T	F	S	S
				1	2	3
4	5	6	7	8	9	10
11	12	13	14	15	16	17
18	19	20	21	22	23	24
25	26	27	28	29	30	31

SEPTEMBER

M	T	W	T	F	S	S
1	2	3	4	5	6	7
8	9	10	11	12	13	14
15	16	17	18	19	20	21
22	23	24	25	26	27	28
29	30					

OCTOBER

M	T	W	T	F	S	S
		1	2	3	4	5
6	7	8	9	10	11	12
13	14	15	16	17	18	19
20	21	22	23	24	25	26
27	28	29	30	31		

NOVEMBER

M	T	W	T	F	S	S
					1	2
3	4	5	6	7	8	9
10	11	12	13	14	15	16
17	18	19	20	21	22	23
24	25	26	27	28	29	30

DECEMBER

M	T	W	T	F	S	S
1	2	3	4	5	6	7
8	9	10	11	12	13	14
15	16	17	18	19	20	21
22	23	24	25	26	27	28
29	30	31				

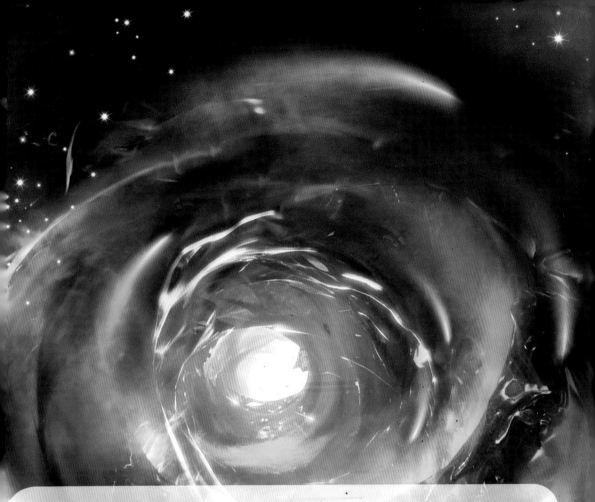

PUBLISHER'S NOTE

Step back in time this year to mark the 50th anniversary of *Doctor Who*, which first aired in black-and-white on the BBC in 1963. Since then there have been eleven Doctors, from William Hartnell to Matt Smith, each one memorable in his own way. Here we present each Doctor in turn with a selection of images from the many episodes, along with companions and the monsters he pitted his wits against, including Daleks, Sontarans, Silurians and Cybermen. Much of *Doctor Who* has been there from the very beginning – from the theme music and swirling vortex effects of the opening credits to his trusty TARDIS and adversaries such as the Daleks and Cybermen. The series has always featured gripping plots to keep viewers on the edge of their seats. The final months of the diary feature episodes from the exciting second half of Series 6, when the Doctor takes on Hitler, Cybermen, nightmare monsters and a hotel full of darkest fears, watches Amy age by the minute after she becomes trapped in a quarantine facility, and finally marries River Song in a bid to correct time and prevent the universe's destruction. Life goes on for the Doctor and is anything but dull!

Doctor Who first appeared on British TV in November 1963, starring William Hartnell as the Doctor. Billed as a family series, viewers were treated to its distinctive opening credits, featuring a swirling vortex, and memorable theme music, composed by Ron Grainer, elements that have remained integral to the series to this day. The Doctor travelled to different planets and time periods with his granddaughter Susan in the TARDIS, a time machine masquerading as a police box, which was much bigger on the inside than it looked from the outside. They are soon joined by two unwilling companions, teachers Ian and Barbara, and it wasn't long before they encountered Daleks and Cybermen. When Hartnell left the series the idea of regeneration was hatched as a way of replacing him with a new Doctor, played by Patrick Troughton.

1960s

31	Monday
1	Tuesday — New Year's Day
2	Wednesday
3	Thursday
4	Friday
5	Saturday
6	Sunday

M	T	W	T	F	S	S	M	T	W	T	F	S	S	M	T	W	T	F	S	S
	1	2	3	4	5	6	7	8	9	10	11	12	13	14	15	16	17	18	19	20
21	22	23	24	25	26	27	28	29	30	31										

JANUARY

Daleks invade London in 'The Dalek Invasion of Earth'

7	Monday
8	Tuesday
9	Wednesday
10	Thursday
11	Friday
12	Saturday
13	Sunday

When we first met him, the Doctor was very much a mystery. He could be charming one moment, grumpy and impatient the next. The first Doctor was always convinced of his own brilliance, and could look down his nose at his human companions, but occasionally we glimpsed his hidden softer side and wicked sense of humour. He wore the formal attire of a gentleman in the early 1900s.

First Doctor
William Hartnell 1963–1966

M T W T F S S M T W T F S S M T W T F S S
  1 2 3 4 5 6 7 8 9 10 11 12 13 14 15 16 17 18 19 20
21 22 23 24 25 26 27 28 29 30 31

JANUARY

The cast on set in the TARDIS filming
'An Unearthly Child'

14	Monday
15	Tuesday
16	Wednesday
17	Thursday
18	Friday
19	Saturday
20	Sunday

Vicki and Koquillion in 'The Rescue', an episode that takes place on planet Dido.

First Doctor
William Hartnell 1963–1966

M	T	W	T	F	S	S	M	T	W	T	F	S	S	M	T	W	T	F	S	S
	1	2	3	4	5	6	7	8	9	10	11	12	13	14	15	16	17	18	19	20
21	22	23	24	25	26	27	28	29	30	31										

JANUARY

The Doctor's granddaughter, Susan, and her teacher, Ian, in
'Planet of the Giants'

The Doctor and clown in
'The Celestial Toymaker'

21 Monday

Martin Luther King Day

22 Tuesday

23 Wednesday

24 Thursday

25 Friday

26 Saturday

27 Sunday

First Doctor
William Hartnell 1963–1966

M	T	W	T	F	S	S	M	T	W	T	F	S	S	M	T	W	T	F	S	S
	1	2	3	4	5	6	7	8	9	10	11	12	13	14	15	16	17	18	19	20
21	22	23	24	25	26	27	28	29	30	31										

JANUARY

Susan and the Doctor come across the Daleks for
the first time in 'The Daleks'

28	Monday
29	Tuesday
30	Wednesday
31	Thursday
1	Friday
2	Saturday
3	Sunday

Susan finds much to be concerned about in 'An Unearthly Child'

First Doctor
William Hartnell 1963–1966

M	T	W	T	F	S	S	M	T	W	T	F	S	S	M	T	W	T	F	S	S
1	2	3	4	5	6	7	8	9	10	11	12	13	14	15	16	17	18	19	20
21	22	23	24	25	26	27	28	29	30	31										

JANUARY

The Doctor examines an old Viking helmet
in 'The Time Meddler'

Space Security Service Agent Sara Kingdom,
who is dispatched to find the Doctor and his
companions in 'The Daleks' Masterplan'

4	Monday
5	Tuesday
6	Wednesday
7	Thursday
8	Friday
9	Saturday
10	Sunday

The second Doctor concealed his formidable intelligence behind a mask of childlike innocence and evasive charm. His shabby, somewhat comical clothes reflected his untidy approach to life. Many of his enemies underestimated this strange little man, always to their cost. He could often be found playing a battered recorder, which he claimed helped him to think.

Second Doctor
Patrick Troughton 1966–1969

M	T	W	T	F	S	S	M	T	W	T	F	S	S	M	T	W	T	F	S	S	M	T	W	T	F	S	S
			1	2	3	4	5	6	7	8	9	10	11	12	13	14	15	16	17
18	19	20	21	22	23	24	25	26	27	28

FEBRUARY

Jamie, Zoe and the Doctor in 'The Krotons'

'The Doctor goes in search of a Yeti in 'The Abominable Snowman'

11	Monday
12	Tuesday
13	Wednesday
14	Thursday
	Valentine's Day
15	Friday
16	Saturday
17	Sunday

Second Doctor
Patrick Troughton 1966–1969

FEBRUARY

Victoria and the TARDIS in
'The Abominable Snowman'

Polly, the Doctor and Ben in 'The Moonbase'

| 18 | Monday |
| | Presidents Day |

| 19 | Tuesday |

| 20 | Wednesday |

| 21 | Thursday |

| 22 | Friday |

| 23 | Saturday |

| 24 | Sunday |

Zoe, one of the Doctor's
companions, in 'The Krotons'

Second Doctor
Patrick Troughton 1966–1969

'Polly and Ben wearing special space suits in 'The Moonbase'

Zoe, the Doctor and Jamie in 'The War Games'

25	Monday
26	Tuesday
27	Wednesday
28	Thursday
1	Friday
2	Saturday
3	Sunday

Dominator Rago in 'The Dominators'

Second Doctor
Patrick Troughton 1966–1969

M T W T F S S   M T W T F S S   M T W T F S S   M T W T F S S
        1 2 3 4 5 6 7 8 9 10 11 12 13 14 15 16 17
18 19 20 21 22 23 24 25 26 27 28

FEBRUARY

The cybermen as they appear in
'The Tomb of the Cybermen'

Toberman, the Doctor, Kaftan and Professor Parry
in 'The Tomb of the Cyberman'

In the 1970s *Doctor Who* was filmed in colour. The third Doctor, Jon Pertwee, spent most of his tenure on Earth, travelling through different centuries rather than to different galaxies and planets. The Doctor had a nemesis in The Master, a fellow renegade Time Lord. The Sontarans made their first appearance in 'The Time Warrior'. Tom Baker took over the role in 1974, and the series became more popular than at any other point in its original 26-year run. Plots became more scary and violent, based on popular science-fiction stories of the day. K-9, the robot dog, was introduced to lighten up the show. Sarah Jane and Leela were among the third and fourth Doctors' many companions.

1970s

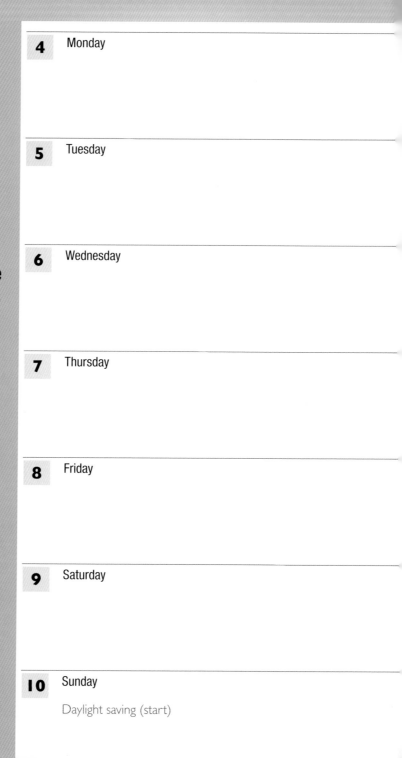

4	Monday

5	Tuesday

6	Wednesday

7	Thursday

8	Friday

9	Saturday

10	Sunday
	Daylight saving (start)

A Sontaran with the Doctor in 'The Time Warrior'

11	Monday

12	Tuesday

13	Wednesday

14	Thursday

15	Friday

16	Saturday

17	Sunday
	St Patrick's Day

The third Doctor cut a dashing figure in his velvet smoking jacket, flowing cloak and ruffled shirt. He was a master of martial arts and took a childlike delight in piloting vehicles of all kinds – helicopters, hovercraft, motorbikes, speedboats. His direct and striking manner could seem arrogant – even rude – but he was fiercely moral, anti-authoritarian, and even given to moments of philosophical reflection.

Third Doctor
Jon Pertwee 1970–1974

M	T	ш	T	F	S	S	M	T	ш	T	F	S	S	M	T	ш	T	F	S	S
				1	2	3	4	5	6	7	8	9	10	11	12	13	14	15	16	17
18	19	20	21	22	23	24	25	26	27	28	29	30	31							

MARCH

The Doctor, Axon and The Master
in 'The Claws of Axos'

18	Monday
19	Tuesday
20	Wednesday
21	Thursday
22	Friday
23	Saturday
24	Sunday

Jo Grant and the Doctor in
the TARDIS in 'Colony in
Space'

Third Doctor
Jon Pertwee 1970–1974

M	T	W	T	F	S	S	M	T	W	T	F	S	S	M	T	W	T	F	S	S
				1	2	3	4	5	6	7	8	9	10	11	12	13	14	15	16	17
18	19	20	21	22	23	24	25	26	27	28	29	30	31							

MARCH

The Doctor in 'Spearhead from Space'

Benton, Yates, the Doctor, Brigadier Lethbridge-Stewart
and Sarah Jane in 'Invasion of the Dinosaurs'

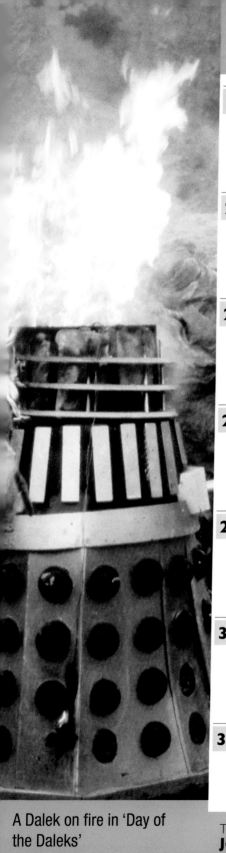

25	**Monday**
	Passover (begins at sundown)
26	**Tuesday**
27	**Wednesday**
28	**Thursday**
29	**Friday**
	Good Friday
30	**Saturday**
31	**Sunday**
	Easter Sunday

A Dalek on fire in 'Day of the Daleks'

Third Doctor
Jon Pertwee 1970–1974

M	T	W	T	F	S	S	M	T	W	T	F	S	S	M	T	W	T	F	S	S
				1	2	3	4	5	6	7	8	9	10	11	12	13	14	15	16	17
18	19	20	21	22	23	24	25	26	27	28	29	30	31							

MARCH

Jo Grant and the Doctor in 'Mind of Evil'

1	Monday
	Easter Monday
2	Tuesday
3	Wednesday
4	Thursday
5	Friday
6	Saturday
7	Sunday

The fourth Doctor, with his wide eyes, toothy grin, mop of curly hair and unbelievably long scarf, could be sombre and silly, innocent and all-knowing, casually friendly and coldly detached. Viewers never knew what this wildly unpredictable character would do next. His clothes reflected his unconventional personality, resembling the shabby elegance of a 19th century intellectual.

Fourth Doctor
Tom Baker 1974–1981

APRIL

The Doctor and Sarah Jane on the planet
of Zeta Minor in 'Planet of Evil'

8	Monday
9	Tuesday
10	Wednesday
11	Thursday
12	Friday
13	Saturday
14	Sunday

The Doctor emerging
from the TARDIS in 'Horns
of Nimon'

Fourth Doctor
Tom Baker 1974–1981

M T Ш T F S S M T Ш T F S S M T Ш T F S S
1 2 3 4 5 6 7 8 9 10 11 12 13 14 15 16 17 18 19 20 21
22 23 24 25 26 27 28 29 30

APRIL

Leela, a warrior of the savage
Sevateem tribe from another planet,
who decides to travel with the
Doctor in 'The Face of Evil'

'The Doctor using a device to decode a
Martian signal in 'Pyramids of Mars'

15	Monday
16	Tuesday
17	Wednesday
18	Thursday
19	Friday
20	Saturday
21	Sunday

Sarah Jane keeps an eye out for Sutekh in 'Pyramids of Mars'

Fourth Doctor
Tom Baker 1974–1981

M T W T F S S M T W T F S S M T W T F S S
1 2 3 4 5 6 7 8 9 10 11 12 13 14 15 16 17 18 19 20 21
22 23 24 25 26 27 28 29 30

APRIL

The Doctor examines an Egyptian sarcophagus in 'Pyramids of Mars'

22	Monday
23	Tuesday
24	Wednesday
25	Thursday
26	Friday
27	Saturday
28	Sunday

An alien Zygon, living beneath Loch Ness in Scotland, plans to take over Earth in 'Terror of the Zygons'

Fourth Doctor
Tom Baker 1974–1981

M	T	W	T	F	S	S	M	T	W	T	F	S	S	M	T	W	T	F	S	S
1	2	3	4	5	6	7	8	9	10	11	12	13	14	15	16	17	18	19	20	21
22	23	24	25	26	27	28	29	30												

APRIL

The first Romana and K-9 in 'The Ribos Operation'

In the 1980s there were three incarnations of the Doctor. A new title sequence was commissioned and the theme music was rearranged by Peter Howell. Peter Davison, the fifth Doctor, was the youngest to play the role and notable for his human-like vulnerability. The sixth Doctor, played by Colin Baker, was controversial because he used deadly force against his enemies in some episodes, something the Doctor had never done before. The seventh Doctor, played by Sylvester McCoy, began playing the role in a comedic style, but he was soon transformed into a darker figure. The series was suspended in 1989 and filming ended. The last episode to be transmitted was 'Survival'.

1980s

29	Monday
30	Tuesday
1	Wednesday
2	Thursday
3	Friday
4	Saturday
5	Sunday

M	T	W	T	F	S	S	M	T	W	T	F	S	S	M	T	W	T	F	S	S
		1	2	3	4	5	6	7	8	9	10	11	12	13	14	15	16	17	18	19
20	21	22	23	24	25	26	27	28	29	30	31

MAY

A Cyberman from 'The Five Doctors'

6	Monday
7	Tuesday
8	Wednesday
9	Thursday
10	Friday
11	Saturday
12	Sunday
	Mother's Day

The fifth Doctor appeared much younger than his predecessors; a fresh-faced, athletic young man, with a passion for cricket and a gentler, more vulnerable character. Endlessly curious, this Doctor ran breathlessly from place to place, often frustrated by a universe which seemed to have no sense of fair play. He wore a cricketer's pullover under an elegant frock coat, with a stick of celery as his buttonhole.

Fifth Doctor
Peter Davison 1981–1984

M T Ш T F S S M T Ш T F S S M T Ш T F S S
1 2 3 4 5 6 7 8 9 10 11 12 13 14 15 16 17 18 19
20 21 22 23 24 25 26 27 28 29 30 31

MAY

'The Doctor and his companions, Adric, Tegan and Nyssa'

13 Monday

14 Tuesday

15 Wednesday

16 Thursday

17 Friday

18 Saturday

19 Sunday

The Brigadier, the Doctor
and Turlough in front of
a Transmat capsule in
'Mawdryn Undead'

Fifth Doctor
Peter Davison 1981–1984

M	T	W	T	F	S	S	M	T	W	T	F	S	S	M	T	W	T	F	S	S
	1	2	3	4	5	6	7	8	9	10	11	12	13	14	15	16	17	18	19	
20	21	22	23	24	25	26	27	28	29	30	31									

MAY

The Doctor, Tegan and Turlough wrestle to maintain control
of the TARDIS in 'Resurrection of the Daleks'

Tegan, Nyssa and the newly regenerated Doctor
explore the Zero room in 'Castrovalva'

20 Monday

21 Tuesday

22 Wednesday

23 Thursday

24 Friday

25 Saturday

26 Sunday

Daleks return to London
to rescue Davros in
'Resurrection of the Daleks'

Fifth Doctor
Peter Davison 1981–1984

M	T	W	T	F	S	S	M	T	W	T	F	S	S	M	T	W	T	F	S	S
		1	2	3	4	5	6	7	8	9	10	11	12	13	14	15	16	17	18	19
20	21	22	23	24	25	26	27	28	29	30	31									

MAY

The Doctor and Kamelion disguised at King John in
'The King's Demons'

27 Monday

Memorial Day

28 Tuesday

29 Wednesday

30 Thursday

31 Friday

1 Saturday

2 Sunday

Peri, a young American
girl, is rescued by Turlough
and taken to the TARDIS to
recover in 'Planet of Fire'

Fifth Doctor
Peter Davison 1981–1984

M	T	W	T	F	S	S	M	T	W	T	F	S	S	M	T	W	T	F	S	S
		1	2	3	4	5	6	7	8	9	10	11	12	13	14	15	16	17	18	19
20	21	22	23	24	25	26	27	28	29	30	31									

MAY

The Doctor, Tegan and Turlough in 'Mawdryn Undead'

3	Monday
4	Tuesday
5	Wednesday
6	Thursday
7	Friday
8	Saturday
9	Sunday

Just like his clothes, the sixth Doctor's personality was an explosion of contradictions. He could appear arrogant and dismissive, and was always ready with an apt quotation or a witty put-down. But here we had a Doctor who cared deeply, and on a massive scale – he always saw the big picture and so could sometimes overlook the more human concerns of his companions.

Sixth Doctor
Colin Baker 1984–1986

M T W T F S S M T W T F S S M T W T F S S
                1   2   3   4   5   6   7   8   9 10 11 12 13 14 15 16
17 18 19 20 21 22 23 24 25 26 27 28 29 30

JUNE

Peri and the Doctor emerge from the TARDIS
after landing in a London scrapyard in
'Attack of the Cybermen'

10   Monday

11   Tuesday

12   Wednesday

13   Thursday

14   Friday

15   Saturday

16   Sunday

Father's Day

Peri receives some cell
mutation treatment in
'Vengeance on Varos'

Sixth Doctor
Colin Baker 1984–1986

M	T	W	T	F	S	S	M	T	W	T	F	S	S	M	T	W	T	F	S	S
				1	2	3	4	5	6	7	8	9	10	11	12	13	14	15	16
17	18	19	20	21	22	23	24	25	26	27	28	29	30							

JUNE

The Doctor in 'The Twin Dilemma'

Sil, an envoy of the Galatron Mining
Corporation in 'Vengeance on Varos'

17	Monday
18	Tuesday
19	Wednesday
20	Thursday
21	Friday
22	Saturday
23	Sunday

A warfaring Sontaran in 'The Two Doctors'

Sixth Doctor
Colin Baker 1984–1986

M	T	Ш	T	F	S	S	M	T	Ш	T	F	S	S	M	T	Ш	T	F	S	S
				1	2	3	4	5	6	7	8	9	10	11	12	13	14	15	16
17	18	19	20	21	22	23	24	25	26	27	28	29	30							

JUNE

The Doctor and Peri in 'Revelation of the Daleks'

The Doctor and Peri head to
Spain in 'The Two Doctors'

24	Monday
25	Tuesday
26	Wednesday
27	Thursday
28	Friday
29	Saturday
30	Sunday

A Vervoid from 'The Trial
of a Timelord: Terror of the
Vervoids'

Sixth Doctor
Colin Baker 1984–1986

M	T	W	T	F	S	S	M	T	W	T	F	S	S	M	T	W	T	F	S	S
				1	2	3	4	5	6	7	8	9	10	11	12	13	14	15	16	
17	18	19	20	21	22	23	24	25	26	27	28	29	30							

JUNE

The Doctor in 'Vengeance on Varos'

1	Monday
2	Tuesday
3	Wednesday
4	Thursday
	Independence Day
5	Friday
6	Saturday
7	Sunday

At first the seventh Doctor appeared to be a comedic character in the 'nutty professor' mould. But his clowning covered a secretive side we had never seen before. An arch-manipulator, this Doctor always seemed one step ahead of friends and foes alike. An accomplished physical comedian, actor Sylvester McCoy was keen to explore the Doctor's darker side.

Seventh Doctor
Sylvester McCoy 1987–1989 and 1996

M	T	W	T	F	S	S	M	T	W	T	F	S	S	M	T	W	T	F	S	S
1	2	3	4	5	6	7	8	9	10	11	12	13	14	15	16	17	18	19	20	21
22	23	24	25	26	27	28	29	30	31											

JULY

The Doctor spends time at a holiday camp
in Wales in 'Delta and the Bannerman'

8	Monday
9	Tuesday
10	Wednesday
11	Thursday
12	Friday
13	Saturday
14	Sunday

The Doctor in
'Remembrance of
the Daleks'

Seventh Doctor
Sylvester McCoy 1987–1989 and 1996

M T W T F S S M T W T F S S M T W T F S S
1 2 3 4 5 6 7 8 9 10 11 12 13 14 15 16 17 18 19 20 21
22 23 24 25 26 27 28 29 30 31

JULY

The Doctor and his new companion Ace, in 'Dragonfire'

15 Monday

16 Tuesday

17 Wednesday

18 Thursday

19 Friday

20 Saturday

21 Sunday

The Doctor and Ace find themselves fighting two factions of Daleks in 'Remembrance of the Daleks'

Seventh Doctor
Sylvester McCoy 1987–1989 and 1996

M T Ш T F S S M T Ш T F S S M T Ш T F S S
1 2 3 4 5 6 7 8 9 10 11 12 13 14 15 16 17 18 19 20 21
22 23 24 25 26 27 28 29 30 31

JULY

The Doctor and Caretaker in 'Paradise Towers'

22	Monday
23	Tuesday
24	Wednesday
25	Thursday
26	Friday
27	Saturday
28	Sunday

Cybermen advancing in
'Silver Nemesis'

M	T	W	T	F	S	S	M	T	W	T	F	S	S	M	T	W	T	F	S	S
1	2	3	4	5	6	7	8	9	10	11	12	13	14	15	16	17	18	19	20	21
22	23	24	25	26	27	28	29	30	31											

JULY

Helen A with Fifi. She ruled a
human colony on Terra Alpha and
appeared in 'The Happiness Patrol'

The Doctor and Ace in 'The Greatest
Show in the Galaxy'

After much speculation, the Doctor made a brief return to television in a 1996 movie, where he was played by Paul McGann. In a return to the original essence of Doctor Who, McGann wore clothes reminiscent of the first Doctor and the Sonic Screwdriver was re-introduced. The interior of the TARDIS was quite different from the stark white, modern appearance of the original machine, and had the appearance of an old-fashioned type of time machine. The seventh Doctor made a brief appearance at the beginning of the movie before he regenerated into the eighth Doctor. A co-production between the BBC and US Network Fox, the movie was filmed in Canada. The storyline featured a race against time to the beginning of the new millennium, when The Master planned to bring about Earth's destruction at midnight on 31 December 1999. Fortunately the Doctor triumphed.

1990s

29	Monday
30	Tuesday
31	Wednesday
1	Thursday
2	Friday
3	Saturday
4	Sunday

M	T	W	T	F	S	S	M	T	W	T	F	S	S	M	T	W	T	F	S	S
			1	2	3	4	5	6	7	8	9	10	11	12	13	14	15	16	17	18
19	20	21	22	23	24	25	26	27	28	29	30	31

AUGUST

The Doctor with Dr Holloway,
also known as 'Amazing Grace'

5 Monday

6 Tuesday

7 Wednesday

8 Thursday

9 Friday

10 Saturday

11 Sunday

He only appeared in one movie-length adventure, but the eighth Doctor made an enormous impact when he burst onto our screens in 1996 for the first new *Doctor Who* story in seven years. For one night only we saw the Doctor reborn as a passionate, daring and fearless adventurer – facing motorbike chases, death-defying escapes and even a savage hand-to-hand battle with the Master, but still finding time for a romantic kiss with the beautiful Dr Grace Holloway.

Eighth Doctor
Paul McGann 1996

M	T	Ш	T	F	S	S	M	T	Ш	T	F	S	S	M	T	Ш	T	F	S	S
			1	2	3	4	5	6	7	8	9	10	11	12	13	14	15	16	17	18
19	20	21	22	23	24	25	26	27	28	29	30	31								

AUGUST

The Doctor at the TARDIS controls in the TV movie

12	Monday
13	Tuesday
14	Wednesday
15	Thursday
16	Friday
17	Saturday
18	Sunday

The Doctor agrees to take the remains of The Master back to Gallifrey, but things don't go according to plan in the TV movie

Eighth Doctor
Paul McGann 1996

M	T	W	T	F	S	S	M	T	W	T	F	S	S	M	T	W	T	F	S	S
			1	2	3	4	5	6	7	8	9	10	11	12	13	14	15	16	17	18
19	20	21	22	23	24	25	26	27	28	29	30	31

AUGUST

The Doctor emerges from the TARDIS

POLICE TELEPHONE
FREE
FOR USE OF
PUBLIC
ADVICE & ASSISTANCE
OBTAINABLE IMMEDIATELY
OFFICER & CARS
RESPOND TO ALL CALLS
PULL TO OPEN

19 Monday

20 Tuesday

21 Wednesday

22 Thursday

23 Friday

24 Saturday

25 Sunday

After being attacked by The Master, the Doctor suffers from amnesia in the TV movie

Eighth Doctor
Paul McGann 1996

M	T	W	T	F	S	S	M	T	W	T	F	S	S	M	T	W	T	F	S	S
			1	2	3	4	5	6	7	8	9	10	11	12	13	14	15	16	17	18
19	20	21	22	23	24	25	26	27	28	29	30	31

AUGUST

The Master attaches a device to the Doctor's head that
resembles a crown of thorns and then attempts to crucify
him above the Eye of Harmony

26	Monday
27	Tuesday
28	Wednesday
29	Thursday
30	Friday
31	Saturday
1	Sunday

The Doctor travels alone in
the TV movie

Eighth Doctor
Paul McGann 1996

M T W T F S S M T W T F S S M T W T F S S
          1 2 3 4 5 6 7 8 9 10 11 12 13 14 15 16 17 18
19 20 21 22 23 24 25 26 27 28 29 30 31

AUGUST

The Doctor at the controls of
the TARDIS

Doctor Who was relaunched in 2005 when Christopher Eccleston climbed inside the TARDIS and set off on a new series of adventures with Rose Tyler. While the outside of the TARDIS looked the same as ever, the inside had had a complete makeover. Set mostly on Earth, the Doctor pitted his wits against foes old and new once again, among them Daleks, Slitheen and Gelth. After one successful season the Sonic Screwdriver was passed to David Tennant, who played the Doctor for a further three series. He teamed up with Martha Jones and then Donna Noble to combat Cybermen, Oods and Weeping Angels. In 2010 Matt Smith became the eleventh, and youngest, Doctor to wield the Sonic Screwdriver in a brand new TARDIS, with Amy Pond as his companion. They were soon joined by Rory, her partner, and River Song, an archaeologist who seemed to know the Doctor well, to face a series of enemies and a quest that began in Utah.

2000s

| 2 | Monday |
| | Labor Day |

| 3 | Tuesday |

| 4 | Wednesday |
| | Rosh Hashanah (begins at sundown) |

| 5 | Thursday |

| 6 | Friday |

| 7 | Saturday |

| 8 | Sunday |

SEPTEMBER

9	Monday
10	Tuesday
11	Wednesday
12	Thursday
13	Friday
	Yom Kippur (begins at sundown)
14	Saturday
15	Sunday

When the Doctor returned to our screens in 2005 he was a changed man – now the last of his kind and the only survivor of the devastating Time War. Haunted by these terrible events, the lonely traveller rediscovered his purpose in life when he met shop girl Rose Tyler and a seemingly unbreakable bond formed between them.

Ninth Doctor
Christopher Eccleston 2005

M	T	W	T	F	S	S	M	T	W	T	F	S	S	M	T	W	T	F	S	S
				1	2	3	4	5	6	7	8	9	10	11	12	13	14	15		
16	17	18	19	20	21	22	23	24	25	26	27	28	29	30						

SEPTEMBER

The Doctor plays with a deck of cards in 'Rose'

The Doctor follows close behind Rose Tyler
in 'The Long Game'

16	Monday
17	Tuesday
18	Wednesday
19	Thursday
20	Friday
21	Saturday
22	Sunday

Jabe, who sacrifices herself to save the Doctor in 'The End of the World'

Ninth Doctor
Christopher Eccleston 2005

M	T	W	T	F	S	S	M	T	W	T	F	S	S	M	T	W	T	F	S	S
				1	2	3	4	5	6	7	8	9	10	11	12	13	14	15
16	17	18	19	20	21	22	23	24	25	26	27	28	29	30

SEPTEMBER

John Barrowman at the controls of The TARDIS

A poster seeking help when Rose Tyler goes missing in 'Aliens of London'

23 Monday

24 Tuesday

25 Wednesday

26 Thursday

27 Friday

28 Saturday

29 Sunday

The TARDIS delivers a message in 'Aliens of London'

M	T	Ш	T	F	S	S	M	T	Ш	T	F	S	S	M	T	Ш	T	F	S	S
								1	2	3	4	5	6	7	8	9	10	11	12	13	14	15
16	17	18	19	20	21	22	23	24	25	26	27	28	29	30						

SEPTEMBER

Autons are activated by the Nestene Consciousness in 'Rose'

Rose and Harriet Jones
meet some aliens in
'Aliens in London'

30	Monday
I	Tuesday
2	Wednesday
3	Thursday
4	Friday
5	Saturday
6	Sunday

Ninth Doctor
Christopher Eccleston 2005

M	T	W	T	F	S	S	M	T	W	T	F	S	S	M	T	W	T	F	S	S
						1	2	3	4	5	6	7	8	9	10	11	12	13	14	15
16	17	18	19	20	21	22	23	24	25	26	27	28	29	30

SEPTEMBER

A monstrous Reaper hovering above a house in 'Father's Day'

The Doctor and a wedding party look on in disbelief
at a Reaper in 'Father's Day'

7	Monday
8	Tuesday
9	Wednesday
10	Thursday
11	Friday
12	Saturday
13	Sunday

The tenth Doctor was irrepressible, a sparking live-wire with unlimited energy who burst into any situation with a cheeky grin and boundless enthusiasm. Here was a Doctor whose mind and mouth worked overtime – effortlessly authoritative and ingenious, with a charm that appealed even to some of his enemies. He suffered great tragedy with the departure of Rose and the return of the Master, but always remained a fiercely moral hero.

Tenth Doctor
David Tennant 2005–2010

M	T	W	T	F	S	S	M	T	W	T	F	S	S	M	T	W	T	F	S	S
1	2	3	4	5	6	7	8	9	10	11	12	13	14	15	16	17	18	19	20
21	22	23	24	25	26	27	28	29	30	31										

OCTOBER

Rose and the Doctor in 'A Christmas Invasion'

The Doctor and Martha Jones travel to Elizabethan
England in 'The Shakespeare Code'

14 Monday

Columbus Day

15 Tuesday

16 Wednesday

17 Thursday

18 Friday

19 Saturday

20 Sunday

Rose does some undercover work in a school cafeteria in 'School Reunion'

Tenth Doctor
David Tennant 2005–2010

M	T	W	T	F	S	S	M	T	W	T	F	S	S	M	T	W	T	F	S	S
	1	2	3	4	5	6	7	8	9	10	11	12	13	14	15	16	17	18	19	20
21	22	23	24	25	26	27	28	29	30	31										

OCTOBER

The Doctor is attacked by Dave in 'Silence in the Library'

Lumic becoming the Cyber Controller in 'Age of Steel'

21 Monday

22 Tuesday

23 Wednesday

24 Thursday

25 Friday

26 Saturday

27 Sunday

Cybermen return to Earth
to attempt to overtake it in
'Rise of the Cybermen'

OCTOBER

Davros returns to lead the Daleks in 'The Stolen Earth'

Donna Noble and her grandfather, Wilfred Mott,
in 'Turn Left'

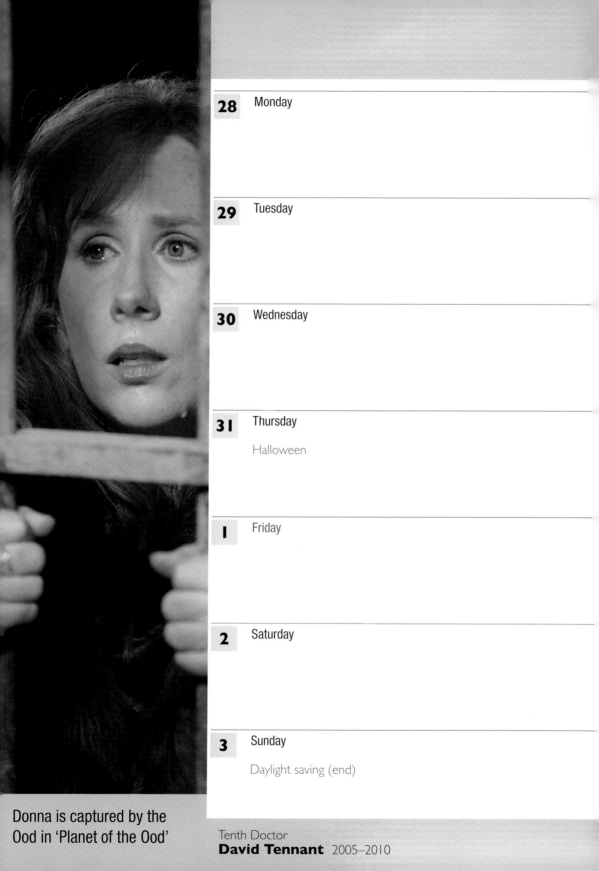

28	Monday

29	Tuesday

30	Wednesday

31	Thursday
	Halloween

1	Friday

2	Saturday

3	Sunday
	Daylight saving (end)

Donna is captured by the
Ood in 'Planet of the Ood'

Tenth Doctor
David Tennant 2005–2010

M	T	W	T	F	S	S	M	T	W	T	F	S	S	M	T	W	T	F	S	S
1	2	3	4	5	6	7	8	9	10	11	12	13	14	15	16	17	18	19	20
21	22	23	24	25	26	27	28	29	30	31									

OCTOBER

In 'The Unicorn and the Wasp' the Doctor and Donna join forces with Agathie Christie to reveal murders by alien wasps and explain why the world's most famous crime novelist will disappear for ten days

4	Monday
5	Tuesday
6	Wednesday
7	Thursday
8	Friday
9	Saturday
10	Sunday

By his own admission the eleventh Doctor is a genius and a madman. He has the same sparking intelligence as his predecessors but it seems to be firing in every direction at once. He has the curious innocence of a child mixed with the ancient wisdom of the centuries. He can seem clumsy and chaotic, but only a foolish enemy would underestimate him. The rumpled tweed jacket, bow-tie and braces reflect his strange mixture of ancient and modern.

Eleventh Doctor
Matt Smith 2010–present

M	T	W	T	F	S	S	M	T	W	T	F	S	S	M	T	W	T	F	S	S
				1	2	3	4	5	6	7	8	9	10	11	12	13	14	15	16	17
18	19	20	21	22	23	24	25	26	27	28	29	30

NOVEMBER

Amy, Rory, River and the Doctor take on the Silence
in 'The Wedding of River Song'

11	Monday
	Veterans' Day

12	Tuesday

13	Wednesday

14	Thursday

15	Friday

16	Saturday

17	Sunday

In 'Let's Kill Hitler' the
TARDIS crash-lands in
1930s Berlin, bringing the
Doctor face to face with the
greatest war criminal in the
universe. And Hitler.

Eleventh Doctor
Matt Smith 2010–present

M	T	Ш	T	F	S	S	M	T	Ш	T	F	S	S	M	T	Ш	T	F	S	S
				1	2	3	4	5	6	7	8	9	10	11	12	13	14	15	16	17
18	19	20	21	22	23	24	25	26	27	28	29	30

NOVEMBER

Amy and Rory in 'Let's Kill Hitler'

18 Monday

19 Tuesday

20 Wednesday

21 Thursday

22 Friday

23 Saturday

24 Sunday

Every child is scared of monsters, but George's terrified pleas for help reach the Doctor. In 'Night Terrors' the Doctor tries to allay his fears, but it won't be easy because George's monsters are real.

Eleventh Doctor
Matt Smith 2010–present

M	T	Ш	T	F	S	S	M	T	Ш	T	F	S	S	M	T	Ш	T	F	S	S
				1	2	3	4	5	6	7	8	9	10	11	12	13	14	15	16	17
18	19	20	21	22	23	24	25	26	27	28	29	30								

NOVEMBER

25	Monday

26	Tuesday

27	Wednesday
	Chanukah (begins at sundown)

28	Thursday
	Thanksgiving

29	Friday

30	Saturday

1	Sunday

In 'The Girl Who Waited' Amy is trapped in a quarantine facility for victims of an alien plague. Can Rory save her before she is killed by kindness?

M	T	W	T	F	S	S	M	T	W	T	F	S	S	M	T	W	T	F	S	S
				1	2	3	4	5	6	7	8	9	10	11	12	13	14	15	16	17
18	19	20	21	22	23	24	25	26	27	28	29	30

NOVEMBER

Old Amy in 'The Girl Who Waited'

Old Amy fights to save young Amy in
'The Girl Who Waited'

2	Monday
3	Tuesday
4	Wednesday
5	Thursday
6	Friday
7	Saturday
8	Sunday

In 'The God Complex' the TARDIS lands in a hotel where every visitor's room contains their deepest, darkest fears. What lies in wait in the Doctor's room?

Eleventh Doctor
Matt Smith 2010–present

M	T	W	T	F	S	S	M	T	W	T	F	S	S	M	T	W	T	F	S	S
					1	2	3	4	5	6	7	8	9	10	11	12	13	14	15	
16	17	18	19	20	21	22	23	24	25	26	27	28	29	30	31					

DECEMBER

An image of a Weeping Angel appears before the
Doctor and his companions in 'The God Complex'

Strange characters appear in the hotel in
'The God Complex'

9	Monday
10	Tuesday
11	Wednesday
12	Thursday
13	Friday
14	Saturday
15	Sunday

In 'Closing Time' the Doctor's final days are upon him, but when he drops in to say farewell to his old friend, Craig, he discovers that the Cybermen are waiting.

Eleventh Doctor
Matt Smith 2010–present

DECEMBER

The Doctor and Craig on the lookout for
a Cyberman in 'Closing Time'

16	Monday

17	Tuesday

18	Wednesday

19	Thursday

20	Friday

21	Saturday

22	Sunday

As the Doctor makes his final journey to the shores of Lake Silencio in Utah in 'The Wedding of River Song', he knows only one thing can keep the universe safe – his own death. But has he reckoned without the love of a good woman?

Eleventh Doctor
Matt Smith 2010–present

M T W T F S S M T W T F S S M T W T F S S
          1   2   3   4   5   6   7   8   9 10 11 12 13 14 15
16 17 18 19 20 21 22 23 24 25 26 27 28 29 30 31

DECEMBER

In 'The Wedding of River Song' the Doctor marries River Song,
and seals the union with a kiss to restart time and keep the
universe from disintegrating. Death is now the Doctor's fate.
Or is he to live in the shadows?

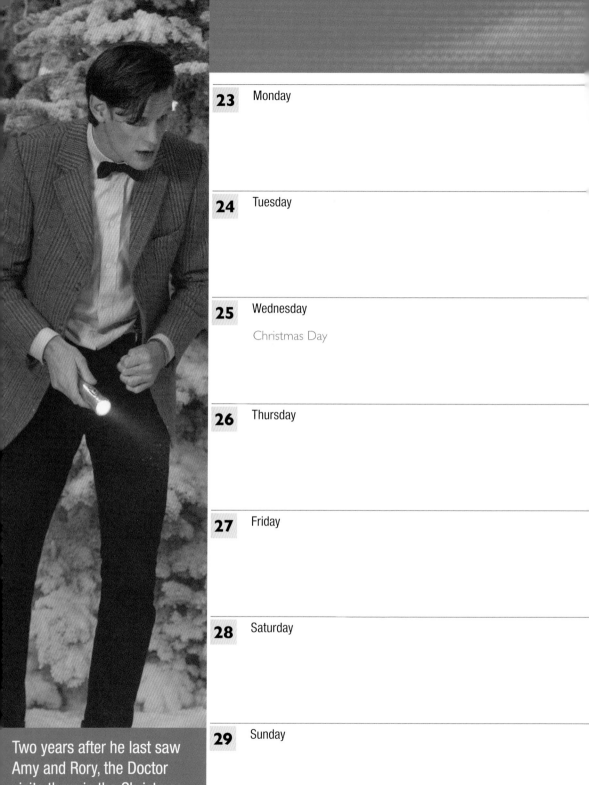

23	Monday

24	Tuesday

25	Wednesday
	Christmas Day

26	Thursday

27	Friday

28	Saturday

29	Sunday

Two years after he last saw Amy and Rory, the Doctor visits them in the Christmas special 'The Doctor, The Widow and The Wardrobe'

Eleventh Doctor
Matt Smith 2010–present

M T W T F S S M T W T F S S M T W T F S S M T W T F S S
                  1   2   3   4   5   6   7   8   9 10 11 12 13 14 15
16 17 18 19 20 21 22 23 24 25 26 27 28 29 30 31

DECEMBER

Cyril opens a present under the
Christmas tree to reveal a time portal
to a snow-covered forest

30	Monday

31	Tuesday

1	Wednesday
	New Year's Day

2	Thursday

3	Friday

4	Saturday

5	Sunday

The Wooden King on his throne in the lighthouse in 'The Doctor, the Widow and the Wardrobe'

M T W T F S S M T W T F S S M T W T F S S
1 2 3 4 5 6 7 8 9 10 11 12 13 14 15 16 17 18 19
20 21 22 23 24 25 26 27 28 29 30 31

JANUARY

The Doctor, Lily and Cyril with the Wooden Queen

Cyril, Lily and their mother, Madge Arwell

Published in 2012 by Mallon Publishing Pty Limited

PO Box 1210 Research Victoria Australia 3095

Produced by Mallon Publishing Pty Limited
Designer Bec Yule @ Red Chilli Design
Editor Margaret Trudgeon
Compilation and design © 2012 Mallon Publishing Pty Limited

Printed in China through Printplus Limited

Distributed in the USA by Diamond Comic Distributors, Inc — located at 1966 Greenspring Drive Suite 300, Timonium, MD 21093